MW01600491

STILL BECOMING

STILL
BECOMING
My Journey Through Fire
and Faith

KAMARA HOPWOOD

STILL BECOMING Copyright © 2025
Kamara Hopwood
All rights reserved. No part of this book should be reproduced electronically,
mechanically (including photocopying), or by any other means without
permission
of the publisher or articles and reviews. Unauthorized copying, posting online, or
distribution of this book in any form is prohibited without prior permission from
the author except for brief excerpts in reviews or articles.
Published by Jamjuds Publishers
https://jamjudspublishers.renderforestsites.com/

i

Dedication

This book is dedicated to the young girl I once was. The one who didn't think she'd make it, Who cried herself to sleep and still woke up to try again. You survived; now your survival has become someone else's strength.

To the God who never left me, covered me when I was exposed, loved me back to life, and turned my pain into purpose. To my mother, whose faith was my foundation and whose prayers were a shield in the spirit. You'll never fully know how many times you saved me.

Thank you. And to every soul who is still walking through the fire— Don't give up. You are not forgotten. You are still becoming.

.

Table of Contents

INTRODUCTION: MORE THAN A STORY V

CHAPTER 1: THE WARNING 1

CHAPTER 2: THE ATTACK BEGINS 10

CHAPTER 3: THE TRUTH REVEALED 17

CHAPTER 4: THE TURNING POINT 24

CHAPTER 5: THE COMEBACK....................................31

CHAPTER 6: PURPOSE PROTECTED 39

CHAPTER 7: STILL BECOMING 45

A LETTER TO YOU, THE READER 53

Introduction: More Than a Story

I did not grow up thinking I would write a book about spiritual warfare someday. I never imagined that I, an ordinary girl with dreams of graduating from school and making something of myself, would come face-to-face with a force so dark it almost took my life. However, here I am—alive to tell the story. Moreover, this is more than just a story. This is a testimony.

This book is my truth. It's the account of a time in my life when evil was sent to destroy me. A time when I was targeted through Witchcraft by someone close to me—

someone I never would've suspected. It's a journey through depression, fear, betrayal, and the silent suffering that almost broke me. Even more so, it's a story about purpose, God's divine protection, and how prayer pulled me back from the edge.

When I was about to enter my final year of high school, I thought I was stepping into one of the most exciting seasons of my life. Instead, I entered into a spiritual war. I was under attack—and I didn't even realize it.

My mother had a dream, a warning from God that something wasn't right, that I wasn't supposed to go to school that day. However, I didn't understand the weight of what she was saying. I told her I had to go. I couldn't let anything stop me from graduating. What happened next nearly killed me. Night after night, I was waking up with panic attacks. At school, I couldn't focus. I was depressed, confused, and suicidal. Teachers grew concerned. My grades began to slip. Then came the truth— I found out that someone in my own family had used Witchcraft against me. That revelation broke my heart and opened my eyes. But it didn't end there. God had the final say.

Through prayer, dreams, divine encounters, and the unexplainable power of grace—I **SURVIVED**. I passed my exams. I graduated at the top of my class. And most of all, I discovered the truth of a word spoken to me in a dream: "You shall not die. You are here for a purpose, and until that purpose is fulfilled, nothing and no one can harm you." If you're reading this, I want you to know— there is no darkness too deep for God to reach you in. There is no weapon that can prosper against what He has anointed. You may not understand why specific battles come your way, but if He's called you, He will cover you.

This book is proof that even when hell tries to silence your voice, Heaven already has the final word.

Chapter 1:
The Warning

I t all began with a dream—my mother's dream. She woke up one morning with a heavy heart and urgency in her voice. She told me I wasn't supposed to go to school that day. She couldn't explain exactly why, but she was sure something wasn't right. "Daughter," she said, "God showed me. If you go to school today, something will happen to you." But I didn't listen.

I respected my mother deeply. Her words always carried weight, especially when it came to spiritual matters. I believed in dreams—especially the ones she said came from God. And yet, there was a part of me that couldn't let go of my plans, my path, and my purpose.

You see, I also believed in my education. I had fought too hard to come this far. Late nights with textbooks, early mornings with swollen eyes, sacrifices upon sacrifices just to stay on top. I was finally entering my final year of high school—the most important year. I had my eyes set on passing all my CXC exams. I wanted to graduate with honors, make my family proud, and set the foundation for a better life. A different life; one where I could rise above the limits that tried to hold me back.

So, despite her warning, despite the way my spirit stirred uncomfortably at her words, I made a decision. I looked her in the eyes and said, "Mommy, I have to go. I'll be fine. Just pray for me." I tried to reassure her, but the truth is, I was also trying to reassure myself. Something inside of me knew this wasn't just about school. It was deeper. It was spiritual. But I didn't want to seem weak, and I didn't want fear to make my choices for me. I thought that as long as I prayed and kept my faith strong, nothing could touch me. But I was wrong.

That day, I didn't just walk into a classroom. I walked into a battlefield. Looking back now, I realize that when God sends a warning, it's not always about protecting your body. Sometimes, it's about shielding your spirit from something invisible but deeply dangerous. God sees what we don't. He sees the hidden traps, the silent attacks, and the spiritual sabotage that's been set in motion before we even open our eyes. But I didn't see it. I wasn't spiritually mature enough to discern the season I was entering. I thought my determination was enough. I thought that if I just held on tight to my routine, everything would fall into place.

But what I didn't know was that sometimes, determination without discernment is deadly. I had no idea that someone had already set a trap for me. Before I even stepped foot on the school compound that morning, the enemy had already laid plans. A spiritual net had been cast over my path—quietly, strategically, deliberately. I didn't see it, couldn't sense it in the natural, but in the spirit realm, something had shifted. I wasn't just walking into a regular school day—I was walking into warfare. And that's when it started.

The first sign was subtle—so subtle that I brushed it off. It was heaviness as if the atmosphere had thickened. The sun was out, but everything felt dim. My classmates laughed, gossiped, and moved about like everything was normal, but I felt out of place, out of sync. I couldn't explain it. I just knew something was off.

It was just past noon when everything changed. A sharp, stabbing pain hit the back of my head. Not like a normal headache—no, this was different. It was sudden, violent, and crippling. It felt like something unseen had struck me with force. I clutched my head, hoping it would pass, but the pain only intensified and then came the confusion.

My thoughts became scrambled. My heart began to race. The classroom that once felt familiar now felt threatening. I looked around and saw the same faces I saw every day, but everything felt wrong. Like I didn't belong. Like I was exposed, and everyone could see it. That moment marked the beginning of something I didn't have the language to describe.

That night, I couldn't sleep. I tossed and turned, drenched in sweat, plagued with anxiety I couldn't trace. When I did fall asleep, I woke up at exactly 3:00 a.m. with a weight on my chest and a presence in my room that I couldn't explain. It was the first of many nights like that. The attacks became relentless.

Every night, I'd wake up at the same hour. My body frozen, my spirit gripped by fear. Sometimes, I'd hear voices, whispers in the darkness, shadows that moved across the wall without light. I'd call on the name of Jesus, and the presence would slowly lift, but it would always return the next night. I was under attack—and I didn't even know it.

I tried to act normal during the day, to keep up appearances at school and home, but inside, I was unraveling. My body was present, but my mind was elsewhere—stuck in a place of fear and confusion. I was drained; I was not just tired but drained. Emotionally, mentally, spiritually. It felt like something was trying to erase me—bit by bit.

I started forgetting things. My schoolwork suffered. I would look at my textbooks and not remember how to study. Words blurred on the page. I knew the answers in my head, but when I went to write them down, my mind would blank. My teachers started to notice. "She's not focused." "She used to do better." "Something's off with her." But no one knew what was really happening. Not even me.

It wasn't until weeks later, when the attacks deepened that I realized this wasn't just a phase or burnout. This was spiritual. Something—or someone—had opened a door, and I was the target. And as much as I tried to pray, I felt like my prayers were hitting a ceiling.

I'd open my mouth to worship, and nothing would come out. I'd try to read my Bible, and the words would vanish from my understanding. I was drowning in silence, suffocating in a spiritual fog. I wanted to cry for help, but how do you explain to someone that you're being attacked by something they can't see? So I kept quiet. And the enemy kept working.

But little did he know—God had already started writing my comeback. Because even in the silence, God was watching. Even in the spiritual fire, God was preserving me. And though I couldn't feel it, He was planting something deep inside of me that would one day rise from the ashes. But first, I had to be broken. Because brokenness leads to surrender, which opens the door to healing, and that's where my real journey began.

Chapter 2:
The Attack Begins

It's one thing to feel off. Tired. Sad. Stressed. But what I was going through was deeper than that. I was drowning—and no one could see it. After that first warning dream from my mother, everything in my life began to crumble.

Piece by piece. Quietly, then all at once. At first, it felt like exhaustion.

A normal kind of fatigue. I told myself maybe I just needed rest. Maybe school had pushed me too hard. But deep down, I knew better. I wasn't just tired—I was hollow. I wasn't just sad—I was being swallowed by a darkness I didn't have words for. I wasn't just stressed—I was under attack.

Every night, I woke up around the same time—3:00 a.m.—my heart pounding, my body frozen, fear gripping me like a vice.
It became a pattern—a haunting. My room, which once felt like a place of safety, became a battlefield. There was a presence—something unseen but very real. It lingered. It watched. It tormented. I'd sit up in bed with sweat pouring down my back, gasping for air, trying to whisper the

name of Jesus. Sometimes I couldn't even get it out. Sometimes, it felt like something was pressing down on my chest, trying to silence me. Panic attacks became my silent enemy. They didn't scream. They didn't warn. They just came—uninvited, unannounced, unrelenting.

At school, I was falling apart. On the outside, I wore my uniform, smiled when necessary, and answered when called—but inside, I was barely holding it together.

No matter how hard I tried to concentrate, my mind wandered. It was like I was watching my life from a distance, unable to catch up.

I knew the answers in class. I could say them out loud. But when it came time to write, it was like something had snatched the clarity right out of my mind. Words came out jumbled. Sentences collapsed on themselves. It was like I had the knowledge but no access to it—a blocked path.

I started to fear myself. I questioned my intelligence. Was I losing my mind? The girl who once had plans to top her class was now hoping to pass. I watched my dreams slip further away each day, and the worst part? I didn't even have the strength to fight back.

My teachers noticed. I could see it in their faces. Concern. Confusion. Pity. Eventually, they called in my mother for a meeting. I sat across from them, quiet and ashamed. They spoke in careful tones, trying not to sound too harsh. "If things don't improve... she may have to repeat the year." Repeat? That word hit me like a punch. As much as I wanted to scream, "I'm trying!" I couldn't say a word. Because no matter how hard I worked, it didn't seem to matter. It felt like something—or someone—was working against me. And still, no one truly knew what I was facing.

Then came the silence—the kind of silence where even prayer feels empty. Where worship feels like dust in your mouth, I prayed. I cried. I begged. But God felt distant. It was the kind of silence that shakes your faith to the core. I started to wonder: Was I being punished? Had I done something wrong? Why wasn't God answering me? The thoughts got darker. Louder. "No one sees you." "No one cares." "You're a failure." "You're alone." "What's the point in living?"

I remember one night vividly. I lay in bed, staring at the ceiling, and asked a question

I never thought would cross my mind: Would anyone miss me if I were gone? It was the scariest, saddest question I had ever asked myself. And the fact that I couldn't confidently answer it broke something inside me.

I thought about ending it all. More than once. It felt like I was disappearing. It was like my spirit was fading out of the world, and no one even noticed. But even in the silence, God was moving. Even when I thought He had left me, He was right there. Even when I was too weak to pray for myself, someone else was praying for me. Even when it looked like the enemy had won—God was still in control.

At the time, I couldn't see it. But He was working behind the scenes, preserving me, shielding me. Even while I slept, angels were fighting for me. The truth didn't come out until later—after I had survived the worst. But what I thought was just stress, what I thought was just anxiety, was something far more sinister.

What I was experiencing was spiritual warfare. An attack that didn't start in the natural—but in the unseen realm. And the worst part? It wasn't random. It was sent. Deliberate. Targeted. Someone had taken my name. Someone had spoken my destiny into the enemy's camp. Someone had tried to spiritually assassinate me before I could step into purpose. And that someone was family.

Chapter 3:
The Truth Revealed

I survived the storm before I even knew what caused it. For the longest time, I was trying to make it through the day. Trying to breathe. Trying to function. Trying not to break. But the truth—the full truth— didn't come until much later. I had already endured the darkest season of my life when the reason behind it finally surfaced.

It was just before I started college. A fresh chapter. A new beginning. I should've been excited. Relieved. Hopeful. And in some ways, I was. But then the truth came out, hitting me like a brick. Someone had taken my name...someone had taken my future and handed it over to the enemy. Witchcraft. The very word sent chills through my body.

Someone had gone to the enemy's camp on my behalf—without my consent or knowledge. Someone had intentionally tried to destroy me spiritually, mentally, emotionally, and academically. That someone was my aunt-in-law. Family by marriage; familiar in face, foreign in spirit.

Present at gatherings, warm in tone, deceptive in spirit.

This was a woman who smiled at me. Who greeted me with kind words. Someone who looked me in the eye and held conversations as if everything was normal. But all the while, behind the mask, she had placed my name on a spiritual altar and laid me before darkness. Assigned destruction to my destiny. And why? Because her daughter—my cousin—had to repeat Grade 11, which placed her in the same class as me.

Somehow, that reality twisted her heart into envy. Somehow, the sight of my progress, my ambition, and my dreams made me a threat. So, instead of helping her child rise, she set out to pull me down. It made no sense. I wasn't competing with anyone. I had no grudge. No ill feelings. I was just a girl with goals, doing her best to build a future for herself and make her family proud. But that's the thing about spiritual warfare—logic doesn't apply. When the spirit of jealousy enters, it blinds people to reason. It convinces them that your light is their threat. And instead of seeking their healing, they seek your harm.

I was in shock. I couldn't wrap my mind around it. This was family. I was confused, angry, and utterly heartbroken. How could someone so close wish me harm? How could someone who shared meals with me, prayed with the family, and pretended to care secretly plot my downfall? It was betrayal wrapped in a smile, a knife hidden behind a hug. But it was also a revelation. A hard one, but a necessary one. That's when I truly began to understand that purpose came with warfare.

You don't get anointing without opposition. You don't carry oil without attracting attack. And the moment you step into your calling, you become a threat—not just to the enemy, but to anyone he can influence.

The devil doesn't always come dressed in red. Sometimes, he borrows the face of someone you love. Someone you trust. Someone whose presence you would never suspect. But that doesn't mean God isn't still greater. As I sat with the truth, waves of emotions flooded me. First pain. Then rage. Then, a deep, gut-wrenching sorrow. But underneath all of it was peace.

Not because what she did was okay—far from it. But because I had survived it.
And not just survive, I had overcome. I realized then this wasn't just about school.

It wasn't just about my cousin or some classroom rivalry. This was about destiny. This was about silencing my voice before I could use it. Breaking my spirit before I could rise. Destroying my mind so I'd never believe I was worthy. But the enemy failed.

Because even though I didn't know what was happening behind the scenes, God did. He saw the hands lifted against me. He heard the prayers prayed in darkness. He knew the intent. He knew the assignment. And He allowed it—for a time—not to destroy me but to strengthen me.

The word says in Isaiah 54:17, "No weapon formed against you shall prosper, and every tongue that rises against you in judgment, you shall condemn." It didn't say the weapon wouldn't form. It said it wouldn't win. And now I know why. Because the purpose was calling me—even in the pit. And even though I had to walk through the fire, I came out refined, not ruined.

Yes, I cried. Yes, I was confused. Yes, I was suicidal. Yes, I wanted to give up. But I didn't. I was bruised, but I wasn't broken. Wounded, but not wasted. Targeted, but not taken out. I had survived an assassination attempt—not against my body, but against my purpose. And survival wasn't the end of the story. Purpose was.

Chapter 4:
The Turning Point

I reached my breaking point. Not the kind people talk about casually—the kind you feel in your bones. The kind that makes your breath shallow, your thoughts heavy, and your body aches even when nothing physically hurts. I was functioning, but I was empty. I smiled, but inside I was withering. No one could see it, but I was unraveling from the inside out.

I felt like I had nothing left to give. No more strength to fight. No more energy to try. No more will to live. The weight of the spiritual warfare, the confusion in my thoughts, and the unseen torment pressing on my chest— it was all too much. I couldn't keep pretending I was okay. I couldn't keep carrying a heart that felt like it was bleeding slowly, invisibly. The worst part? I didn't know how to explain it. How do you tell people you're drowning when they think you're still swimming?

I started to withdraw—not out of pride, but survival. It was easier to be alone than to feel misunderstood. It was easier to isolate than to explain something I couldn't even name. And then came the dream. The one that shifted something deep inside me, the one that saved me.

In the dream, my mother and I were walking together. Everything around us was dark—heavy, like night had settled over our souls. But I could still see her. I looked at her with tired, defeated eyes, and with the kind of honesty only pain can produce, I said: "Mommy, I can't do this anymore. I don't think I'm going to make it." Even in the dream, I meant it. I didn't say it for sympathy—I said it because I was finished. I felt like death was near. Not just physical death but the death of everything I had left inside. My hope. My future. My fight; gone.

But then suddenly, something holy entered the dream, like a light piercing through the dark. Angels appeared. Not the soft, glowing kind from paintings. These were fierce. Radiant. Strong. They looked like authority clothed in glory. Their presence didn't just shift the atmosphere—it commanded it.

One of them stepped forward and looked directly at me. His gaze went deeper than my face—it saw my soul. And then he spoke. Words I would never forget: "You shall not die. You are here for a purpose. And until that purpose is fulfilled, nothing and no one can harm you." It felt like Heaven itself had just placed a seal over my life.

The moment he spoke, something inside me cracked open—not in pain, but in awakening. I woke up gasping for air as if I had been pulled out of drowning. And for the first time in a long time, I felt something I hadn't felt in months: Hope. I didn't jump out of bed fully healed. I didn't suddenly feel like everything was perfect. But something had shifted. I felt seen. I felt covered. I felt chosen.

That dream became my lifeline. My turning point. It reminded me that Heaven still speaks even when the world goes silent. Even when the people around you don't understand your pain, God knows every detail. Even when the enemy tries to convince you you're alone, angels have already been assigned to you.

From that night forward, I began to fight again. Not perfectly. Not without setbacks. But I fought—with prayer. With tears. With Scripture. With worship. I started pressing in, even when I didn't immediately feel God's presence. I learned to pray not just for deliverance but for strength. I learned to worship, not because everything was fine, but because worship reminded me who was still in control. And something powerful began to happen: The darkness started to lose its grip.

I began to recognize when the enemy was whispering lies—and I replaced them with truth, taking every thought captive to the obedience of Christ, just as 2 Corinthians 10:5 commands. I learned that feelings can lie, but God's promises never do. And even in my weakness, the Lord was fighting for me.

My mother's prayers became a blanket of protection over me. There were nights when I couldn't speak a word, but I'd hear her praying in the other room, calling my name, declaring life and cancelling assignments of death. Slowly, I began to believe again. I started to dream again.

And I began to live—not just survive, but live purposefully. That's when I fully understood: The power sent to destroy me could never match the purpose placed inside me.

The turning point didn't mean the battle was over. But it meant I now knew who I was. I now knew whose I was. And I knew that no witchcraft, spiritual attack, or plot from the enemy could ever cancel what God had already written. I had entered a new season—not because everything changed outside, but because something was reborn inside me.

Chapter 5:
The Comeback

It's one thing to survive a battle. It's another thing entirely to come back stronger. Survival is quiet. It's hidden. It happens in the dark—when no one sees the tears, the prayers, or the moments you talk yourself out of giving up. But a comeback? A comeback is a declaration. It says: "Yes, I was broken—but I healed." "Yes, I was attacked—but I rose." "Yes, the enemy tried—but he failed."

After the dream with the angels, something inside of me reignited. God had lit a match in the middle of my darkness and whispered, "Now watch what I do." I wasn't completely free yet but had something I hadn't felt in a long time: Hope.

I didn't know all the answers. I still had hard days. But I knew this one thing: I would not go back. I couldn't let the attack define the rest of my story. I couldn't allow what had been done to me to stop what God wanted to do through me. So I pressed in.

I prayed—not because I felt strong, but because I knew I was weak. I cried—not because I had given up, but because crying became my form of worship. I would sit alone, sometimes in silence, and whisper, "God, please... help me." And every time I did, His peace would meet me—softly, quietly, but faithfully. The panic attacks didn't disappear overnight, but they lost their power. The confusion in my mind began to lift like a fog slowly rolling away with the sun's rise. I started sleeping better. I started breathing deeper. I started believing again.

And that's when I realized I was healing.
Not just physically or emotionally—but spiritually. My focus returned. Slowly but surely, my mind began functioning like it used to—sharp, alert, clear. I was able to read and retain it again. I could understand lessons again. I could study without the mental warfare choking me.

I threw myself into my books—not out of fear but of freedom. I wanted to reclaim the time that had been stolen. I wasn't just studying for grades anymore—I was reclaiming everything the enemy tried to take from me and then came CXC exams.

I walked into each exam room with trembling hands but a steady spirit. I wasn't the same girl who almost dropped out months earlier. I was a different version of myself—battle-tested and spiritually armoured. I didn't just want to pass. I wanted to prove to myself, the enemy, and Heaven—that purpose wins.

When the results came in, I almost couldn't believe it. I didn't just pass. I excelled.
I graduated at the top of my class. Some moments in life feel surreal—moments when you stand in victory and remember

every scar it took to get there. That was one of those moments.

I held my results in trembling hands, and I wept. Not because of the grades—although they were amazing. But because of what they represented. They weren't just scores on a page. They were proof. Proof that God had kept me. Evidence that the prayers worked. Proof that weapon formed against me could not and did not prosper.

I walked through the fire—and not only did I survive, but I came out carrying the evidence. The scars, the wisdom, the strength—they are proof that God was with me. Just as Isaiah 43:2 declares, 'When you pass through the waters, I will be with you; and through the rivers, they shall not overflow you. When you walk through the fire, you shall not be burned, nor shall the flame scorch you.' I didn't just make it out—I emerged refined, like gold tested in the fire.

What was meant to consume me, God used to prepare me. What was meant to drown me, He used to deepen my trust. I was not the same as before the fire—I was stronger, wiser, and more rooted in purpose. His presence didn't just protect me; it transformed me.

Walking across that graduation stage wasn't just ceremonial—it was spiritual. With every step I took, I felt like I was reclaiming the years the enemy tried to steal. I wasn't just holding a diploma. I was holding my testimony. I stood there, wearing that cap and gown, knowing I was more than just a student. I was a survivor. A warrior. A living, breathing reminder that God's power is greater than any witchcraft, any depression, any lie from the enemy.

The same hands that tried to pull me down were now powerless. The same people who doubted me now had to watch what God was doing. The same enemy who wanted to bury me was forced to watch me rise.

That's the thing about purpose: It doesn't crumble under pressure. It doesn't vanish in the fire. It grows in the very soil where the enemy tried to plant your destruction. I had come back. Not perfect. Not untouched. But whole.

And I knew then—I was never just fighting for a grade, a title, or recognition. I was fighting for a purpose. I was fighting for legacy. I was fighting for the destiny God had written for me long before I stepped

onto the battlefield. And the most powerful
part? I won.

Chapter 6:
Purpose Protected

When you walk through the fire, you don't come out the same. You may survive it, yes—but survival changes you. You walk differently. You see differently. You believe differently. The flames may not have burned me physically, but they scorched away illusions, pride, and comfort. And what remained was something stronger.

In the quiet after the storm, I began to see what I couldn't see before: God had been protecting me all along. I wondered, "Where was God when I cried myself to sleep? When I couldn't breathe through the panic? When I thought about ending my life?" Now I know. He was right there. Not always speaking, but always present. I am not always stopping the storm but always standing in it with me.

God didn't just protect me from physical danger—He protected something even more valuable: My purpose. The truth is, the enemy wasn't after my mind just for the sake of it. He didn't care about my school performance simply because of my grades. He wanted to derail the calling on my life.

He tried to silence the voice God had placed in me. He wanted to crush the confidence, the passion, the anointing that would one day set others free.

He wasn't fighting me because of who I was at the time. He was fighting me because of who I was becoming. And that's how the enemy works—he sees hints of the glory God placed inside you and tries to kill it before it matures. Like Pharaoh ordering the death of baby boys in Egypt. Like Herod hunting down baby Jesus. The attacks came early because the purpose was that powerful.

But what the enemy failed to account for was this: God's purpose cannot be cancelled. Not by jealousy. Not by Witchcraft. Not by depression. Not by fear. Through every moment of confusion, through every sleepless night, through every whisper of death and despair—God's hand stayed on my life.

I remember sitting on my bed in silence one night after the worst had passed. There was no music. No tears. Just me and the weight of everything I had survived. And in the stillness, I heard the quietest whisper in my heart: "You were never alone." And I wasn't. God had been orchestrating my protection in ways I couldn't understand at the time:

He gave my mother dreams that revealed the attack before it consumed me. He sent angels in a dream to declare that I would not die. He strengthened me through prayer even when I felt too weak to pray for myself. He exposed the source of the Witchcraft so that it could be broken. Every step. Every breath. Every breakthrough was not random—it was divine strategy. God wasn't reacting. He was leading. He didn't just rescue me but preserved the essence of my calling.

That season of warfare taught me something that no classroom, sermon, or book could teach: Purpose is not something you stumble into. It's something Heaven protects. You don't have to be perfect to be chosen. You don't have to have it all figured out. You have to be willing—and God will do the rest. He'll guard and guide you when necessary and fight for you when you can't fight for yourself.

And when God puts His hand on your life, nothing can remove it. Not envy. Not spiritual attacks. Not even your brokenness. I don't feel fear when I look back on those dark days. I feel faith. I feel gratitude.

Because I know what I survived wasn't just a bad season—it was a battle for destiny. And I didn't just make it out. I made it out on purpose. For purpose. With purpose.

Every scar I carry now testifies to a God who sees, a God who shields, and a God who sustains. I was never just a girl going through a hard time. I was a chosen vessel under fire. And now I walk with the quiet confidence of someone who knows this: "If God be for me, who can be against me?" (Romans 8:31) I am here on divine assignment. I always was. And nothing—no weapon, word, or work of darkness—can stop what God has written over my life. Purpose protected. Purpose preserved. Purpose activated.

Chapter 7:
Still Becoming

Surviving the storm was never the end of the story—it was the beginning of something greater. The battle I faced before my final year of school wasn't just about passing exams or staying afloat. It was spiritual. It was strategic. The enemy attempted to derail the calling God placed on my life before I was even born.

But what the enemy didn't know was that every attack would only deepen my dependence on God. Every setback would fuel my surrender. Every night would prepare me to carry the light. I didn't just make it through—I was transformed. There's a difference between surviving and rising. And I rose. Not because I was strong but because God's strength carried me when I couldn't stand. He lifted me when my soul was too heavy to move. He whispered hope when the silence of depression tried to crush me. I came out of that season changed. Refined. Awakened.

When God allows you to walk through fire and come out refined instead of burned, you don't walk the same. You don't see the world the same. You don't live to please people or prove anything. You live with purpose. You pray with power. You speak with boldness. And you carry a fire that can't be quenched—because you know what it costs to burn and survive.

That season didn't destroy me—it delivered me. It delivered me from pride. From people-pleasing. From spiritual complacency. From self-doubt. And from the lie that I had to earn God's love. In the fire, I met a version of myself I didn't know existed: The warrior. The worshipper. The woman of faith. The daughter of God who would rise from the ashes with clarity, purpose, and authority.

Now I understand why the warfare was so intense. The enemy saw my potential long before I did. He tried to silence the voice that was called to speak life. He tried to smother the light that was called to shine in dark places. But he failed. Because God stepped in—and where there were ashes, He gave beauty.

Today, I walk in purpose—not perfectly, but intentionally. I know that my life isn't just for me. My story is for the unseen. The unheard. The broken. The ones who cry silently at night and wonder if God still sees them. The ones who feel like giving up but choose to stay one more day.

I'm here to tell you: You are not forgotten. You are not forsaken. You are not finished. If you're in the middle of your storm, I've been there. If you're questioning your worth, I've asked those same questions. If you're feeling spiritually attacked, I've fought those invisible battles. And I survived—not because I had all the answers, but because I reached for the God who did. I held on when everything in me wanted to let go. I prayed when I didn't have the strength to speak. I cried out in the dark and discovered that even there, God was present. He met me in the fire. He fought for me in the spirit. And when the dust settled, I realized I wasn't just surviving—I was being shaped, refined, and becoming. So, if you're still in it, don't give up. Your pain has a purpose. Your storm won't last forever. And the same God who pulled me through will pull you through, too.

Moving forward, I no longer carry fear—I carry fire. Not a fire of rage or revenge but a fire of revival. The fire that heals. The fire that reveals purpose awakens identity and lights the path for others. I carry the pillar of fire that led the Israelites through the wilderness—God's presence guiding me through every dark place.

I carry the consuming fire that purifies and sets my soul ablaze with holiness and passion for His presence. I carry the devouring fire that fights for me, breaking chains, tearing down strongholds, and silencing every enemy of my destiny. And I carry the refining fire—the fire that tested, shaped and proved that what God placed in me is stronger than anything I walked through. I walk boldly now, not because I know what tomorrow holds, but because I know Who holds me and that His fire goes before me.

I am still becoming, healing from some wounds and rising from some falls. I am still learning how to let go and let God. But

I'm no longer who I used to be. I'm stronger. Wiser. Marked by mercy and chosen by grace. And if there's one thing I've learned, it's this: When your life is surrendered to God, no attack can erase your anointing. No season can stop your calling. And no weapon formed against you will ever prosper. Because purpose, real, God-given purpose, is protected. And this? This is only the beginning.

Prayer

Lord, I thank You for every fire You've brought me through and every purpose You've preserved. I surrender my journey—my pain, my past, and my process—into Your hands. Refine me, shape me, and complete the work You've started in me. I trust that no experience will be wasted and that every battle will be used for Your glory. I am still becoming, and I walk boldly into what You have destined for me.

I declare that I am chosen, covered, and called. I am not defined by my scars—I am marked by grace. Every setback was a setup

for my testimony. I carry fire, not fear. I walk in purpose, on purpose, for purpose. And this—this is only the beginning.
Amen

A Letter to You,
The Reader

Dear Reader,

If you have made it to the end of this book, I want to thank you—from the deepest part of my heart. Thank you for walking with me through the fire, holding space for my story, and letting my words sit with you in the quiet corners of your life. You didn't just read my pain—you honoured it. You saw the purpose woven through every page.

I didn't write this book for attention or pity. I wrote it because I know what it feels like to suffer in silence. To carry invisible wounds. To be under spiritual attack and have no language for it. I wrote it because someone out there—you, maybe—you are standing in the middle of a storm right now, wondering if they'll make it through.

If that someone is you, please hear me clearly: You are not crazy. You are not weak. You are not invisible. And most of all—you are not alone. The intensity of your battle is proof of the weight of your calling. The fire you're walking through isn't meant to consume you but to refine you. What you're carrying is powerful. And that's precisely why the enemy is afraid of you.

So don't give up. Don't bow to fear. Don't believe the lies that say you're too broken, behind, or far gone. You are still becoming, becoming stronger. Becoming wiser. Becoming the version of yourself that hell tried to stop but Heaven preserved. Let this book be a witness—a living testimony that

God still delivers, protects, heals, and uses ordinary people for extraordinary purposes.

If He brought me through, He will bring you through, too. Hold on. Your story is still being written. With all my love and boldness,

- *Kamara Hopwood*

Made in the USA
Columbia, SC
21 August 2025

61616443R00039